# THEY DON'T KNOW ME

SMOOTH CONTROL

authorHOUSE®

*AuthorHouse™*
*1663 Liberty Drive*
*Bloomington, IN 47403*
*www.authorhouse.com*
*Phone: 1 (800) 839-8640*

*Published by AuthorHouse 03/16/2017*

*ISBN: 978-1-5246-8453-2 (sc)*
*ISBN: 978-1-5246-8452-5 (e)*

*Print information available on the last page.*

*This book is printed on acid-free paper.*

They say the early bird catches the worm.........While the early bird is getting the worms I am in your nest getting your eggs scrambling back to my nest shaking the crows and buzzard's along the way, with the two five tucked revolving automatically everything around me. I am all ready......

Life began for me at the age of five. I remember the first day of elementary school. My mom was dropping me off. I remember looking up at her and she said do you know your way home? I looked at her and said yes. My mother told me once school was out to come straight home. She told me she would see me later. As my mother was leaving the school I looked around me and notice all the other children were crying for their mothers.

I smile and it is on….

My family and I are living in the Potrero Hill Housing Projects. It is me, my dad, mom, two sisters, and four brothers. I am second from the last child. To me I don't know if life is good are not but I can smell something is bad in this spot where we are living. It smells like roach spray and gas was coming out of the heater and vents. It is so bad to me I don't think I am going to live long. I feel if I don't get out of here soon I don't know how long I will live. I feel like I am going to die if we stay here any longer.

I remembered I would always have bad dreams while living in the housing projects. I will never forget this one nightmare I had one night. I dreamed that the devil was standing over me while I was asleep. The image in my dream was a red figure with horns, a long tail holding a black pitch fork. In this nightmare the devil stuck me right in the ass with his pitchfork. I remember I yelled out telling the devil don't let me catch you!!!! I told myself I was going to get that dam devil in my dreams and anything that looked like a demon.

One day my dad came home and said we are moving to a new home. We are leaving the projects. We moved when I was about six years old. We lived in San Francisco. We moved to an area called Lakeview.

It is a new world for me. My family and I lived on Vernon Street which was a very big hill. It was hard to play on that hill. At the bottom of the hill it was flat and it was a dead end.

The dead end was wide open it was a whole new world. It was a lot of kids that lived around the hood. So day by day I began to roam around different parts of the neighborhood. I see more things going on in life than I had ever seen before. It is a lot of things to see and do in this new place.

I am going to school up the hill from where we live. My new elementary school is Jose Ortega. My brothers, sisters, and I would play in our backyard sometimes. It wasn't a huge backyard but it was cool. Our backyard had a lot of trees. One day I was in the backyard by myself just fooling around playing and I heard something. It was someone throwing something at me, if felt like small rocks or something. I later found out it was a small rock being shot from a slingshot. The kid that was shooting the rocks at me was a Chinese boy, who was laughing at me. I picked up a rock and let him have it, and now I am laughing at him. It was someone next door from the guy in the another tree throwing shit too. So now it's on. Rock fight!!! The next day we are at school, we hooked up an laughed about our rock fight the day before. The Chinese guy was Jon Li and the boy next door who was in the tree next to Jon was black Jack. That was his nickname. Damon, another neighborhood kid was also throwing rocks at me. Damon lived about four houses up from Vic.

We became good friends after that. We began going places and seeing things all over the city of San Francisco.

We started hustling candy at school. We would go to the store and buy sunflower seeds,and all kinds of candy, like Boston bake beans, lemonheads, jawbreakers and bubble gum. We would then break them down into five cent bundles. We would be making change. One guy would run to the store at lunch time and re-up on the goods. The rest of us would be in school checking change. I was dime sharp and nickel slick and that is how I was making a dollar out of fifteen cents.

After school we would be hanging out on the dead end street messing around sliding down the hills on cardboard boxes, riding rollercoasters, skateboards, and riding bikes. We would all be having big fun. This is the

60's and it is a lot of shit going at the dead end. It is 50 to 100 kids on the block from the block at all times. We all live in homes in this part of town. It is no housing projects. Where we live there are a lot of trees and a lake on brotherhood way. Me and my crew started building forts in the trees on brotherhood Way. The trees were so thick you could not see the highway going down to the lake. More and more people started coming around. There was this one guy on the dead end who lived behind this big red fence. He would come outside on a skateboard kicking it and being cool. He was mixed with black and white. He lived with his sister, mom, and stepdad. I had never seen his real dad before. This kid name was Matt McMillan. Me and Matt would be in his backyard sometimes playing around. Matt built a three-level tree house in his backyard.

He did not let everyone in his backyard. The highest level of his treehouse was like a crow's nest. When the wind would blow the trees would rock back and forth. We were at the very top of Matt's tree house blowing in the wind.

One day Matt tells me he is going to be in the movies. I said to him what movie are you going to be in? Matt says to me the movie is called the "San Francisco Cable Car Murder". I say to him you don't know anyone who's going to put you in the movies. He said to me, my dad is going to put me in the movies. I said right… your dad don't make movies, he said my real dad does. I said ok, I will see. A little time goes by, one day he came back around the hood and he said I made that movie. I said you didn't make no movie, he said do you want to go see it? So me and a couple of more guys go see the movie. Then Mario said see you fools could have been in the movie. Matt started going to Los Angeles with his dad a lot, who was Chris McMillan. At this time in my life I did not have any hero's, no one to look up to far as a positive role-model. We lived in a day and time where we didn't live in the south and it was different for us in the bay. In the south blacks were still running from the KKK. Me and my crew was not scared of none of that, the south stereo type shit. Where we lived it was all different color races now, it just wasn't white and black.

Time goes on and me and some other guys are starting to get into fights on a daily, on the dead end. These guys are from across the way and are trying to take over the fort. I ain't havein it!!

So I get about ten guys and tell them to come with me. I am going to show you fools how to ride on somebody. I ride. I got fools running back across Brotherhood Way. My boys see I am not playing in the 60's. At this time the Vietnam War is going on. In the news papers all you see are soldiers posing with bloody body parts with the look of death in the soldiers eyes. All I can think about is I wouldn't want to be one of those guys. So on the streets everyone wants to fight each other because this is all you see on the television, magazines, and newspapers. I see men coming home from the war and they are different. They are not who they were when they left. The look in their eyes is scary to me. A lot of these guys are drinking heavily and doing heroin. It was a whole new different time. Things were changing all around me.

So more and more people are starting to came around the block. Time is going by.

The 60's are like the black and white years, nothing seems too bright, no color is in anything. A lot of kids are starting to get high on cheap alcohol, pills, weed, and heroin. So it is what it is, I smoke cigarettes, drink alcohol, and I am smoking weed. As time go by and shit is changing, the 70's come and everything is getting bright. The hippies, its psychedelic time, and free love. Everyone coming out of the 60's. It's all about peace and love.

Now shitis not to be played without here. Shit is moving, the world is moving and I am all in. These days and times a lot of kids are starting to come around the crew now. It could be 100, 50, even 20 of us hanging out together. During this time some of us were able to get our parents cars, so this allowed us to go to different parts of the bay. We would kick-it on Fridays and Saturday nights. The crew and our new friends would go to a liquor store or supermarket and house shit, so we could go and have a party or even a picnic. Going to skating rings was the thing back then and that is what we did. We would bring the party wherever we went. Whoever was around the party was with it.

Real money is on my mind and it is on. My father worked in the Fillmore district in San Francisco. He started a construction company with some Italian guys. They had the money but he did the work. The company was called Lewis and Merlo Construction Company. It was located on Grove and Divisadero Street. After work my dad would go down the block to Hayes and Divisadero Street to his partner shoe shop. His partner was Mr. Bell. Mr. Bell was my homeboy Don grandfather. Mr. Bell could make you a pair of snakeskin, crocodile, or lizard skin shoes. Sometimes when I was on that side I would go into the shoe shop and wait on my dad to come through so I could get a ride to Lakeview. Don also had an uncle, named Herbert Bell. Herbert Bell was a kingpin in Fillmore. Herb sold all the heroin on a spot called the razor. Herb used to come through the shoe shop with bags of money sitting in the back of the shop counting it and talking big shit about where he was getting his money from. As they say the game is sold not to be told, but if you are like me you would sit back open your eyes and ears and get all the game for free. So one day while Herb was counting his money he asked "what you doing young blood"? I told him I was waiting on my dad to come through so I could go home. Herb and his family lived a block over from me and my family. He said I am going that way you want a ride home. I said, yes. On the way home he said I am not going straight there but I am going if you want to ride. So I get in the car with Herb. Along the way we stopping at different places. Down on Fillmore Street, he is getting out the car and getting back in with bags in his hands. So I just sit back and watch him. While I am watching him, he looks like a paperboy on a paper route. Everywhere he goes he is getting money. As we get close to the hood he tells me anytime I think about making money to check him out. We stop by a store on Victoria, it was called Victoria market. Herb goes into the store and comes out with two fifths of Remy Martin. He gets back in the car and opens one up and pours into a white cup. Herb passes me the cup and he said drink this. Herb told me this is what bosses drink. He said I will see you later. I get out the car and walk to the house. When I get home I sit back thinking while I am feeling the Remy. At this moment I am thinking about my oldest brother Scott. When we moved to Lakeview, Scott brought the heroin game with him. So, I was thinking about how to make money from his product. In the morning me and my other brothers would get for school but before we went, Scott would have 20 to 30 album covers laying all over the room covered with heroin. Me and my brothers would form an assembly line, one would scoop the product into the balloon and the other brother would take the balloon and twist it into a knot and put it into a bag. My younger brother would take the bags and count how many balloons were in each bag. While we were doing this we would be checking money. People would be knocking on our garage door to get served the product. Now the garage was one of our bedrooms. My father converted it when we moved in. From that point on I started keeping extra for myself on the side. So I started my own paper route. I wasn't getting a lot of money at first. It was a lot of older dudes on the streets trying to keep me from getting money. From that point I start to get a crew going. A lot of the homeboys in the hood family members was on that shit. So it was easy to get money from the neighborhood.

During this time Matt McMillan came back on the block talking about a movie he and his sister, Ashley made about their dad. It was called "Sweet Sweet Back". He was me and my friends how he was having sex with a lady in the movie. He started laughing and said it was not real sex because she had on a body stocking. We all started laughing. One day he was gone again.

I started using people around me to do different things, because everyone was not the same. A lot of dudes in the hood were square at first. I am about 150 pounds. I am using my muscles for everything in my way. It would not matter if you were 300 pounds, I didn't give a fuck. Do not disrespect me at all. I am not havin it from no man or woman. I am not letting anyone get in my way.

I am all ready getting serious in my life. It is 1973 and I am 15 years old. I am sitting on Randolph Street watching the world watch me. My spot is on some church steps between Victoria and Head Street. I am sitting smoking weed and havin a drink by myself. At this time I was a street commando and Brigadier General. People are all around me, and they think I am a fool. I don't fuck with no one so don't fuck with me.

People started asking me, "do you got it"? I said ask no more. Now the streets are watching me get it. To a lot of people what I was doing was bad, but in the streets it was all good. There was a gym not far from where I lived, named Ocean view gym. Everyone was selling there, but there was no one selling drugs where I am at in the hood. Down here were I am, I am over here going one for one, now it is going everywhere I go, whatever I got. I tell god to tell the devil I'm coming through the gates of hell and I am going it be tearing shit up along the way until he let me go. So until then it's on. Now I ride.

One day I am at Byxbee park and there is an og dude we all know named Bob. He had an old 1967 caddie in front of his house. It had been in front of his house for about three years. I had a partner named Ron., who had a brother named Jake who was about fourteen at the time. Jake asked Bob what was up with his Caddie. Bob gave the car to Jake. The car did not run so Jake pushed it around the corner. I watched Jake literally break the motor down and in about a month later he put it back together again. After that it was on. Jake had me put the battery in and close the hood, the car started right up. I could not believe it. From that day on Jake and I bought cars fixed them up, rode in them for a while, and then sold them. Brought, trade, fix-up and sold.

Now, if you are with me and you do what I do we hustle all day long. We are deep now on my side. If you know me and money and would want to get like me I am doing dirt by myself. Getting it. You can see by the way I look I am Hollywood and I ain't California dreamin in the bay.

I am 16 and I got shit that 50 year old man got and it's a lot of hating going around. The days and times are changing out here on the streets. On the streets now the ogs think they are super fly. All they want to do his snort coke, drink and talk to women. So now dudes my age thinking they can get into the pimp game. Everyone around think they are a pimp. So now I am messing around with different families in the neighborhood. I hook up with two brothers, big Mike and Buzzy Ross. They call them the Ross boys. Mike was about 5'8 and 300 pounds. Buzz was 7 feet 400 pounds. One day me and my brother

Harold were coming home from school. Harold would always tell me about Big Mike in school and how he was a bully. One day me and Harold walking from school yard toward Victoria Street, big Mike was outside his leg was broken so he was on crutches. Mike started talking shit to my brother Harold. I told Harold his leg is broke he could get him. So big Mike started swinging his crutch and hits my brother. I grabbed big Mike arm and kicked him in the leg. Mike start hollowing and crying for his mother. He was yelling he was going to get me, over and over again. So me and Harold started laughing and left. I see big Mike the next day. Mike told me I was cool because no one else never tried to do anything to him. So we laugh, smoked weed, and was partners from that day on.

I don't care, I just continue to be me. I have been selling heroin and weed since the age 13. Mike and Buzz had an uncle who was in the game. His name was Billy. Billy liked me. Billy liked me as if I was his son. Billy used to call me pimping Don but I wasn't a pimp. I just knew how to keep the game going around the old dudes. I would keep a girl around them to throw off their game. So now I am getting street game from Billy. Bill is a Mack, a real Mack, and he was showing me how to be nothing less than that. So now that I am around Mike and Buzz we getting money, for real. We are riding in Rolls Royce's, 6 clean Cadillacs, and a Jag.

It's 1976 and I buy my first ounce of coke for $2500. I take that ounce and make five by packing it up an rolling over the product and making it back hard in a 70 coup Cadillac.

Now I am doing it like an og. On my side of the hood from Brotherhood Way to Ocean Ave, and from 19th Ave to Orizaba Street the game is going and the streets know it is good in the game.

I got a crew of goons with me an everybody is eating. One of my boys name Gerry have a brother in-law name Oscar. He is a little youngster but he see big game in me.

Oscar always came and kicked game so I let him in my game. He was already down.

I don't let know one get in my cars. I am so low out here I don't mix my game with too many people. If I do, it's got to be good. Oscar got game. He is running the young dudes in the hood. Now we are moving all over the bay doing what it do. I have my right hand man Dave, we are all from the same cloth. Time is moving, things are changing, its some new shit in the town, its call freebase. Before this day and time it wasn't no one on the street saying they were homeless, but now this freebase is on the streets and got people out on the streets all night, even days, chasing a high and getting money. This crack shit started to break up families, but the government put it out there. They were running the shit and this made a lot of people become homeless. Me, Dave, Oscar, Jim, Fred, and Ant Nibols would control and patrol the area from sun up to sun down getting our money on. So the next day we would hook up wounded, which means high to the fullest of our precious cargo we carry. We would also exchange war stories about the fools coming through trying to take stripes from somebody that night. Some of us would steal be licking our wounds, which mean still getting high. The same shit is going on day by day.

The og's that are in the game ain't moving no work out of their spots. They are sittin back blowing their brains out. No time to go get money, just sitting back getting freaked by the dope head women. Now I am going on all the paper routes getting paid.

It is the 80's now and the world is going crazy now. Everyone is coming to get money from the streets. Everybody want to be a drug dealer. Now all the square dudes are coming out like roaches trying to get this street money. You got fools out all-night getting money and not going home because they are out on the streets getting high on coke.

So now you know the hood. I am in this money and getting it out of million dollar spots. Back in the day growing up in the 60' and 70's people would come from other parts of the city and call us punks. Because we lived in houses they assumed we were punks. Because they lived in projects they felted they could come into our neighborhood and punk us. These fools did not know me and all the other kids in the hood was from the projects. So we protected our side of the hood. I show them how not let to fools come in and do anything they want to do. I got a crew of misfits and goons. We ready!!

Now me and Oscar is like Eric B. and Rakim moving the crowd making the shit happen on my side of the town where I work at. It aint no stopping, it is just popping. The game is going and we working it. So now on the streets it's a lot of different nationalities. We have people from Jamaica on the streets trying to tell people about the "conscious movement" of the Rastafarians. So we got people in the hood turning Dred and we got people from Iraq, Iran, China, Japan, and Mexico. Now everyone is trying to get money on the streets because they see that the drug game on the street is how everyone is making money. Now that lady is here, Ms. Lisa Kulka her and her crew are on the streets now.

Back in the day the street game came from your family. It was always someone in your family that was in the game doing something. If it was selling dope, or hustling something, it was to make money to help the family. So this is where a lot of the street game came from back in the day. Now it is a new day and time. Around this time I am getting more cars and I hooked up with another home boy, his name is Charles Pierre. Charles got a lot of cars too and his family is in the game. So me and Charles we get cars,

We are hustling and making money. It's around 1984 and I find an old 1965 Cadillac Coupe De Ville convertible.

I seen it on the other side of town in the Mission District. I look at this car for 10 years. It was sitting in someone's yard in the Mission district.

I go and get my boy Jake fresh now. Jake starts it up and I ride. The car is smoking real bad now. I drive through the hood. Now it is a big hold in the top of the roof. You can see through the hole in the seat to the ground.

So I am driving though the hood and see one of the homeboys name Don, and he is laughing telling me he would not pay me to get in that car. I ride, I laugh at him and keep it moving.

In six months I come driving through the hood in a silver and grey drop caddy it was the cleanest car in the bay. I bought the car for $300, and now it looks like a millions dollars.

I see Don and he see me, I tell him to get in, he gets in. Don ask me where did I get this car from. I responded saying, actually it is the same car you told me you wouldn't pay me to ride in. Don then tells me you really got your money on man, let me go and get my money on man.

Don went hustling and got a 67 white on white drop coupe. My boy Don spent 20 thousand dollars on it. He was getting it too in the hood.

It is 1985 and things are getting bad around here. Shit is cracking around here it is and it is real money in the hood and now you can see it.

You got folks from different families coming in trying to do things and it aint going to work.

Not here on my block. So I just sit back in my Cadillac in the back seat with window down on both sides, about three inches. So you can talk to me but you cannot get in. We are already eating and the crew is real hungry and not playing. I continue to sit in the back of my Cadillac and get it.

One day I am coming through the hood and one of my Chinese boys see me.

He tell me to stop an let me holler at you. So I stop and he get in the car. I lethim get in and he start telling me about his ancestors. He said to me,

one day it was like bright lights were coming from the sun, coming down from the sky to the earth.

It was a man on a dragon. It was one of the most beautiful places on earth but the people in this part of land were real poor. They did not know how good they had it here. So, he showed them how to get riches out of this land and he showed them how to protect the land. One day people came to the land and they thought that they could take over; but the man from the sky was an emperor he had took many kings land and riches from them and showed the people of the land how to live peaceful.

The emperor had made all the people around him respect him and everyone around him.

One day you are going to do all you can do here and you will leave from here not to return he said to me you are that man. God be with you my brother. Now as I sit back and get it, I watch the hood go wild.

It's some new shit cheap dope called crack that out now. Now the people on the streets are smoking coke and its going crazy. It is so much money out here you do not want to go home, so its on 24-7. Now everybody is getting it and if you were not you would want to. If you see what the hood is having it looks like you are in Europe now. Everybody is driving foreign cars now. You got a lot of boys on ninja motorcycles that are running hard and it looks like China too.

So now if you get money you better be a beast. If you are not, don't come out at Night. It is a new world outside. People are starting to come up missing or come up short by the gaffelers and maybe even get gaffeled by the police.

Now the feds are in the hood. Too much money is out here and it's getting to be no respect for your game. The og's are trying to get you out the way or the youngsters are trying to kill you for what you got.

So I set back and still move shit and stay out of the way. I am in beast mode myself at all times.

Now you cannot trust your friends. The streets are talking and it aint right.

One day in 1985 I get caught up in the game. I go to the pen. I was not state raised.

Most of my boys had been in an out of jail all of their lives. Not me. So it's going down.

When I enter the state prison I immediately go into boss mode. I hook up with my crew and go to work. I spend my days inside the walls, hustling the pen and anybody around me. I stay in my position and watch my own back. It is not easy inside the pen but I am trying to make it as easy as possible for me.

As I pace my way around a four corner room in my mind I am at peace. I have dreams about flying high in the skies. I know I am high because I am feeling it, and my head is in the clouds

I am looking down at the hawks catching fish taking them back to nest feeding their young's. I think I am free but I am not. It's just another day gone and another wiped tear from my eyes.

I know one day I will be free. It's coming.

It's 1990 and I am free from the gates of hell to return to the streets. It's a new day and time, now shit aint the same. I know who I am now but all the shit I had is gone. It's no more I am letting street life go. It's new faces in the game on the streets now. It's not worth being out there anymore. The money aint shit, and everybody telling on you. So I can win without the streets. I get out of the way. It's a lot crews out on the street now and they are called the "new jacks". Speaking of the "new jacks", one day I am driving down the street heading towards my lab on Randolph and Vernon Street. I am about to drive up the block. I am in my 1966 Chevelle. On the corner of the block is Matt McMillan and I think it was his son who was in the movie with him and one of his boys. Matt had just made the movie New Jack City. I look at him, he look at me. I wanted to talk to him but at this day and time you could not stop on the streets. It was hotter than Hot August Night in Reno. So I throw up the duce's and drive up the hill. Matt don't know at this time the hood is hotter than New Jack City. I am like

Nino Brown and the feds are watching. So I keep moving. So now I am out on the streets, my younger brother Ryan and his partner Dustin and Juan are telling me how the game is different. They telling me to watch myself and the people that are around me because it is not the same out here. Now these dudes are hood rich. It's not easy to get money like it was before. When I went to jail I had money and Jewels. Ryan and Dustin used to call my jewels "Mr. T" started kit. I had eight rings on my fingers, and bracelets on my wrist, fifteen gold chains around my neck. Now everybody wearing "donkey ropes", two and four finger rings on their hands and driving custom made cars. Cats telling me the game don't work like it used to so don't get in.

It's 1995, and one day my brother come and get me from the San Francisco. Times is bad and money is bad for me too.

We are yin yang twins. I am dark and he is light. He is calm, and I am sense. He knows me and he tells me to come to Fairfield, California. So I did. My brother tells me I can get a job and get paid the same day. I said cool, I'll go.

The job sends me to Rio Vista, Ca. I was out in the cow field, where sheep lived and I was looking at the water, and at the fish jumping. I am saying to myself it smells like money. It's on again. I am working construction. I am building steel frame homes, getting real money.

Little do people know I have been working all of my life, well sense I was 16. I was working with my government number. Plus I learned the construction game from my dad when I was out of high school. I worked at the San Francisco International airport.

I got out the pen in 1990. When I got out of the pen, I became a chef at the royal exchange restaurant in San Francisco for eight years.

In Fairfield me and my brother open a grill and deli restaurant by Travis Air Force Base and I was a cook at Travis Air Force Base. Now I am doing construction. I do my own thing on the side. I open up my own cleaning business, Forever Clean, cleaning houses, and construction sites. I also open a moving business called, Keep It Movin.

One day I am at the construction site getting hell of flat tires on my truck, I come up on an invention a high pressure hose for your car. I did patent it. Its call the Equalizer. I upgraded it the Equalizer to the Equalize-Plus.

It was in 1996 by the year 2000 the street game in Northern Cali is bad. All of the work is garbage and you aint getting no real money no more out here.

The coke game is about gone. It's some new old shit. It is called meth. This got the people worse than crack. Oh shit, look out world I ain't in it man. It's your world.

So as I am sitting back thinking of a lot of things I have been through in life, I think I am falling off to sleep. All of a sudden I am hearing a loud panting I think I am waking up but I don't know the panting is getting louder. So as you know if you have been in the underworld you change like a camion so I hit the ground. I slide closer to the sound, as I can see it's that devil. He is on top of someone, he is devouring her. Chewing her up like he was a lion and I didn't if he is hurting her or not. It is a woman I have been seeing for a long time from a far. Every time I tried to get close to her she would disappear. I think it is the devil's girl. I looked at him, and his ass is in the air. The devil tail is sticking straight up at the moon. I see his pitch fork leaning against a stone rock. I slide to the stone and grab the pitch fork and before he could turn his head, I stick in dead in the ass. The demon turns to me and hollers like a beast that just got wounded in the jungle. He yelled to me in a loud and demanding voice, "get the hell out of here now"! I don't look back, I can see the light and I walk toward it. All I know is that I am delivered from hell and all the evil with it. Thank God.

I am living in Contra Costa county now things are going for me out here. If you know me, anything I touch I work. Now I am working on houses and cars. Its 2008 now and the house game is bad to it, aint paying.

My life goes on out in this world and aint nobody giving you nothing. I am working out here doing maintenance work at housing complexes to keep it going and that is bad. So I go to selling old cars. I open up a spot with one of my old school boys from back in the day. He is my boy William Gordon. He is about old school cars too. William and I name our shop Prime Auto Sales. We work trying to keep the bread on our tables.

Its 2016 and I am still here with the grace of god delivered from all evil and live gods way.

One day I am with my family at dinner. While we were eating, my family was talking to their cell phones asking the cell phone question about what celebrities got the most money.

I said to them I bet you $100. 00 that Siri don't know me.

They researched, Siri don't know me. I win.

I wasn't street raised. I raised the streets.